CONTENTS

Black & white photos:
   Aaron Norman 8, 54
   Ken Lucas:Steinhart Aquarium 5, 9, 12, 16, 17, 24, 25, 34, 35, 42, 43, 46, 48, 49, 50, 51, 55, 72, 73, 76, 80, 81, 88, 92
Color photos by the author (17) and Burkard Kahl (8)

Front end paper: A poison-arrow frog, *Dendrobates auratus,* from Panama. Photo by George Dibley.

Back end paper: A hylid frog, *Agalychnis annae,* from Costa Rica. Photo by George Dibley.

Title page: *Pyxicephalus adspersus*, the pixie or South African bullfrog, is one of the few aggressive frogs; it has bony tooth-like projections on the lower jaw and is carnivorous.

Originally published in German by Franckh'sche Verlagshandlung, W. Keller & Co., Stuttgart/1978 under the title *Tropische Frosche.* First Edition © 1978 by Franckh'sche Verlagshandlung.
© 1979 by T.F.H. Publications, Inc. Ltd. for English translation. A considerable amount of additional new material has been added to the literal German-English translation, including but not limited to additional photographs. Copyright is also claimed for this new material.

`TRANSLATED BY HOWARD HIRSCHHORN.

ISBN 0-87666-9267
KW-028

Distributed in the U.S. by T.F.H. Publications, Inc., 211 West Sylvania Avenue, P.O. Box 427, Neptune, N.J. 07753; in England by T.F.H. (Gt. Britain) Ltd., 13 Nutley Lane, Reigate, Surrey; in Canada to the book store and library trade by Beaverbooks, 953 Dillingham Road, Pickering, Ontario L1W 1Z7; in Canada to the pet trade by Rolf C. Hagen Ltd., 3225 Sartelon Street, Montreal 382, Quebec; in Southeast Asia by Y.W. Ong, 9 Lorong 36 Geylang, Singapore 14; in Australia and the South Pacific by Pet Imports Pty. Ltd., P.O. Box 149, Brookvale 2100, N.S.W., Australia; in South Africa by Valiant Publishers (Pty.) Ltd., P.O. Box 78236, Sandton City, 2146, South Africa; Published by T.F.H. Publications, Inc., Ltd., The British Crown Colony of Hong Kong.

TROPICAL FROGS

by HELMUT ZIMMERMAN

Two small tropical American tree frogs, *Phyllomedusa lemur*, very appropriately called lemur frogs.

This black, white and red 'lacquered' *Dendrobates histrionicus* is one of the most beautifully colored poison-arrow frogs.

Kaloula pulchra, of Southeast Asia, is fairly common. They sometimes get into human habitations and eat the insects there. The black-and-white striped reed frog *Hyperolius marmoratus taeniatus* appears in many variants; some are uniform in color, others are striped and both types can differ in shading and pattern.

Introduction

Our urge to collect things knows no limits; we can put together a collection of shells or stones or old porcelain in glass cases and joyfully contemplate it all day every day, and we can even collect colorful and bizarre creatures such as tropical frogs. . .but that involves much more than merely viewing them like museum pieces. If you want to keep tropical frogs just to look at, then you'd better put this book aside. It's a book all about intensive work with these creatures, an activity which helps relieve the stress of your daily run-of-the mill routine work. It includes a chance for

Dendrobates granuliferus, a small poison-arrow frog with rough skin.

Hyperolius marmoratus, a reed frog from East Africa.

tranquil observation, scientific study and also an opportunity to record a whole world of strange sounds. We'll get a look at living wildlife from distant places. . .from the luxuriant green of a lush primeval forest with its hopping, climbing and croaking community of frogs in all the colors of the rainbow. . .or from the dry grass and foliage of the open steppes populated with a myriad of tiny frogs, all resonating loudly with their vocal sacs in a breathtaking frog concert instructively orchestrated as part of their mating ritual. For hobbyists who prefer more tranquility, there are the somewhat primitive tongueless frogs who amble around quietly among the roots and water plants in an aquarium. Their abrupt tumbling movements make them the clowns of the frog world. Their tadpoles are hatched right out of the skin of their backs! Here's a piece of real nature right in our living room, smack in the middle of a noisy metropolis. . .strange little creatures who completely depend upon us. Keeping animals is not only a hobby, it's a responsibility.

We have to take good care of our wards, but because we're animal lovers we gladly accept the task and are the happier and richer for it. Because we're dealing with tropical frogs, these color-rich diamonds, these pearls of the animal kingdom, we have to be particularly careful. They are, unlike other pets, hard to find in the pet shops. Some are quite sensitive and delicate. Unlike our domestic varieties, however, they don't need to hibernate, so they can be kept nicely all year in a terrarium in the living room, where, when the room temperature is turned up just a bit, you can approximate the average temperature of their natural habitat, the tropics.

The tree frog genus *Agalychnis* from Central America contains green-backed frogs with vertical red or yellow iris. *Agalychnis annae* (upper photo) has blue flanks and thighs. The Surinam toad, *Pipa pipa*, (lower photo) is a strange-looking clawed frog with very much reduced eyes.

Bufo blombergi, the Colombian giant toad, feeding on a mouse.

Hyla rufioculis, a lively small tree frog from South America.

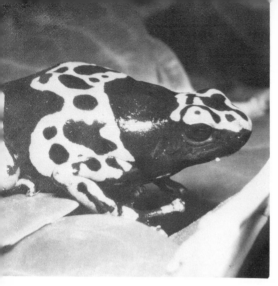

One of the many poison-arrow frogs, *Dendrobates leucomelas* has a dark shiny skin decorated with spots and bands. The width and shape of the bands and the size and number of the spots vary from individual to individual. A close-up view of the head and forelimbs of *Rhacophorus leucomystax* (below). The family Rhacophoridae is related to the family Ranidae.

The Tropics

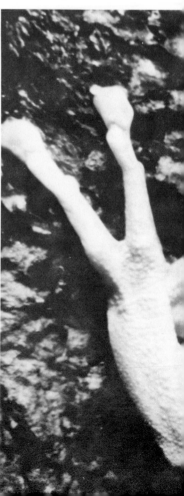

For us frog hobbyists from the cooler regions, the tropics are a dream land, almost a paradise. Never any ice or snow, only sun and warmth, especially moist warmth. Everything is green and blooming, growing and lush the whole year, year in and year out, a real paradise for frogs, with plenty to eat. But other animals, too, need food. Tropical frogs are probably part of their menu! To live in the tropics means a tough battle for life and a battle with all available weapons. Poison is one of these weapons. In the moist heat of the tropical rainforest, small bright red frogs the size of your fingernail climb over tree stumps and foliage in broad daylight. Other frogs related to these tree and foliage climb-

Hyperolius sp., one of about 170 reed frog species.

Centrolenella (upper photo), the glass frog, gets its name from the transparent skin of the belly. The generic name of Australian tree frogs is no longer *Hyla* as they are placed in a separate genus, *Litoria*, hence this is *Litoria peronii* (lower photo).

19

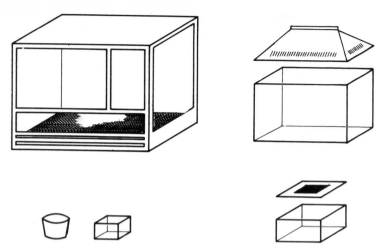

Different types of insect breeding cages.

Plan of an insect breeding cage.

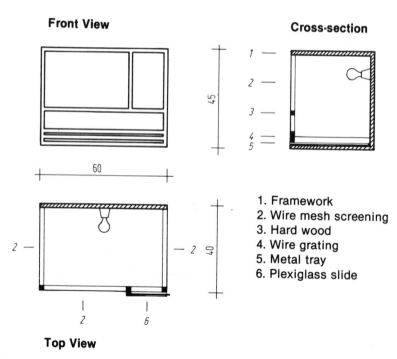

Front View

60

45

Cross-section

1 —
2 —
3 —
4 —
5 —

2 — — 2

40

2   6

Top View

1. Framework
2. Wire mesh screening
3. Hard wood
4. Wire grating
5. Metal tray
6. Plexiglass slide

ers—yellow-black ones, yellow-green ones, blue-yellow ones, or frogs decked out in other vivid colors—likewise show no fear of daylight. These colorful frogs have no enemies who want to eat them, for the poisonous secretion of their skin seems to be feared and respected by would-be predators. Non-poisonous ghost and tree frogs, however, have to live more dangerously, climbing around the foliage at night, and even then cautiously.

Why these green creatures of the black tropical night need such bright red feet and hands, popping red eyes and blue-yellow striped sides is another of nature's secrets. Light green, almost transparent "glass frogs" hop around the cooler mountain lakes, where the air temperature is quite different from our idea of the tropics. For these frogs heat or dryness would be certain death. There is still another habitat in the tropics in which heavy rains occur only about once a year—the savannah, where small marbled frogs sit on the tall grass blades or dry branches in the searing heat. . .where we would almost be done in by the heat. Even in any shadows we might find, the thermometer would still show 104° to 122° F.!

These tropical extremes extend north and south of the equator, that is, between the Tropic of Cancer and the Tropic of Capricorn, or about from 30° north latitude to 27° south latitude. Here, daily temperatures range from 50° to 122° F., with a relative humidity between 40 and 100%. Although we can't really pinpoint by latitude the habitats of all tropical frogs, this is at least the area that interests us the most. It encompasses 40% of the earth's surface, and there the frog population is larger or more varied than in our temperate region. If we want to reproduce tiny sections of this tropical world, then we've got to understand something of the biological factors involved so that we can properly care for our frogs.

Another Australian tree frog, *Litoria caerulea.*

Dendrobates pumilio, the strawberry dendrobatid.

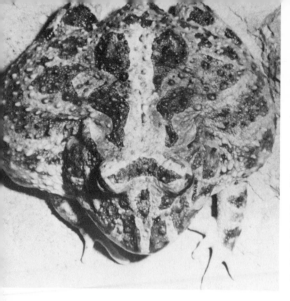

Ceratophrys calcarata, the Colombian horned frog, is a forest dweller whose color and pattern blend well with its habitat. This species can be kept successfully in a terrarium and will not need a constant supply of water in a pool. The giant toad *Bufo marinus* (below) is a well known species and has been introduced to many tropical areas of the world; they are considered a nuisance in Florida.

Terrarium Types

We'll never be able to reproduce, of course, the whole natural habitat of our frogs in a small terrarium. Yet, because of the smaller territory of smaller creatures such as tropical frogs, we're much more able to care for them than for say, birds or monkeys. When we realize just how far a bird flies or how far a monkey ranges every day, we'll realize that caging such animals in a room is forcing life imprisonment upon them. We should mention, also, the "death-row" sort of tiny glass bowl (with its "cute" ladder inside) that some people used to buy or make at home for a pet frog. Such an unnatural solitary confinement is a terrible mistake to be avoided . . . for the frog's sake as well as for ours.

Hemipipa carvalhoi, the dwarf pipid. The tadpoles are already coming out of the skin on the back of the female.

Based upon the frog's natural habitat, here are three basic types of containers: (1) aquarium, (2) partially moist terrarium, and (3) tropical terrarium. One condition is essential for all of these: water must be available, either over the whole floor or as a mini-lake (in the form of a depression in the floor or else simply a shallow container like the lid of a jar).

The size of a terrarium depends upon the number and size of frogs in it, for we'll soon see that a good diet leads to quite a clean-up job! A rule of thumb for the minimal size of terrarium is the distance a young frog can cover in one leap. Longer-than-wide terraria are best for aquatic and ground frogs, while squarish but high ones are better for tree frogs.

An aquarium without any special setup (except that used in a healthy, attractive aquarium, of course) is the simplest home for aquatic tropical frogs. They don't need any aquatic plants, but if you want that decor, then use tough, resistant water plants. Some hobbyists build up a stone wall against the inside of the tank's back wall, then plant that with bog pine roots, etc. You should provide a simple shelter, which the creature especially appreciates during its resting period. You can make a cave out of natural stones (but solid enough to resist being tumbled apart) or else place a clay flowerpot (with its bottom broken out) upside down on the bottom of the aquarium. Put an inside filter behind these "buildings," although this doesn't quite eliminate the need for an occasional water change. Fine gravel or coarse sand makes a good bottom. Cover the aquarium well, for these frogs can leap out or climb up the inside walls and escape. You'll find them later—dried up like mummies—when you clean house! The Spartan setup in an aquarium has an advantage: the frogs can be easily checked up on. You'll have a better chance not to miss the big event when the newborn babies climb out of the skin on the *Pipa* mother's back. But then you've got to quickly fish

28

out the little ones before their parents gobble them up. In larger aquaria, you can mix frogs and fish (large robust ones which stay in the middle or near the surface . . . if the frogs don't eat the fish or vice versa). Feeding this frog-fish combination is not as much a problem as keeping the tank clean, for frogs drop a lot of "fertilizer."

The partially moist terrarium is mostly for savannah frogs. Its construction is like that of a tropical terrarium and differs only by its larger aeration vents and interior setup. A terrarium which is constantly exposed to moisture should not be wooden, but glass, rust-proof metal (like aluminum) or plastic. The necessary heat is provided by pre-heated air from outside the terrarium, a bottom heater, a type of appliance that radiates a mild warmth, or merely a slightly higher-than-normal room temperature. Some water is, of course, necessary, whether over the bottom (with a drain) or only in a lid from a jar. Good cross-ventilation, too, is a must. You can make a small opening at the bottom of one of the narrower sides and a vent on the top at the opposite side, diagonally across the terrarium. The whole top, if it's covered with mesh, can be the vent.

Daylight is best for animals and plants. (Don't make the mistake of using artificial daylight lamps 24 hours a day, for that is quite unhealthy.) If possible, place the terrarium near a window (but not right against it because freezing weather would then be dangerous) with morning light to take advantage of normal daylight hours.

You can even put the terrarium outside to take the sun from time to time (but watch out for the "greenhouse effect" of overheating and stifling), for frogs love to sit out in the sun. Your pet shop can show you artificial daylight lamps for use if you simply cannot put your terrarium anywhere near real daylight. Ordinary garden soil is good for the terrarium bottom, perhaps with a nice mossy cover over it. Besides the bog pine roots, which don't rot or mold, there are also various grasses and leafy plants such as iris,

Gastrotheca marsupiata. Note the elongated toe used for cleaning the 'knapsack' of this marsupial frog.

Atelopus varius is a colorful short-toed frog-like toad that comes in many different colors and patterns.

snakefoot, spineless aloe and sansevieria. It's especially attractive and educational to make your frog's "home away from home" as nearly like that other, natural home as possible insofar as kind of bottom, stones, wood and plants go. But such simulated habitats are not always that easy to make and require some research into the literature on the subject. There is one consolation, however, if you can't create a replica of your pet's natural habitat: most frogs sit as happily on a common *Scindapsus* as on the most expensive *Vriesea*. And many frogs even find the glass of the terrarium a comfortable roost, as long as they can have their nightly bath.

These tenants of your tropical terrarium, however, need more than just a bath; they need air with high humidity, warmth and a well-ventilated terrarium. And there's the hitch, for the moister and warmer the terrarium, the thicker the condensation on the glass, and there goes our clear view of the frog's mini-jungle. Good cross-ventilation not only keeps down any molds that might try to gain a foothold, but also cuts down on the need for so much humidity. The golden mean is best left to the individual hobbyist, who hopefully will develop a feel for just the right combination of all factors. We can only give the technical aspect there. Higher humidity can be obtained by gradually reducing the opening of the ventilation vents to a minimum. Many frogs, like the tree and leaf climbers, accept that quite nicely. Another method consists of evaporation. Install an adjustable heating element in the water container, but don't let the frogs come into contact with that heater. The best solutions are more expensive: (1) a climatized showcase arrangement (such as used for keeping orchids), (2) a bottom heater and adjustable ventilation, or (3) a small greenhouse designed for use in a room.

If you're a good tinkerer or gadgeteer, then you might build a sprinkler or irrigation system controlled by a hydrostat and growth-promoting illumination controlled by a dimmer and timer. There are no limits to your imagination . . . a tiny stream kept running by an aquarium pump . . . a waterfall over rocks . . . a tranquil tributary of the stream providing a nice pond for bathing and spawning . . . roots, moss, or a cork wall covered with bromeliads . . . almost anything you're capable of conceiving and building is possible. Naturally, you've got to keep it all policed and clean, like cleaning out the remains of any creatures you feed to your frogs. Unlike real nature, your terrarium has its limits of self-cleaning. It's too small for that, and you don't really want a *real* "green hell" in which each creature is another's meal. We'll go into this subject of eating, especially about live foods, now (and after that we'll discuss a subject of interest to us as keepers of rare creatures, the subject of breeding and rearing).

A terrarium suited for the frogs from tropical rain forests.

Atelopus varius, a short-toed frog from Central America, is a colorful but small species. They are available commercially but require a supply of live insects for food. The genus *Kassina* (*K. weali* is pictured below) is just one of the many true frog genera found in Africa. These frogs feed on termites, lepidopterans, flies, etc.

Feeding

Most frogs try to eat almost anything that moves and is smaller than their mouth. But we want to exclude frogs and their relatives as food for other frogs, for in some countries many kinds are protected by law. There are many other foods. Mealworms (beetle larvae) shouldn't be given exclusively of other foods, but only as a supplement. We can buy them easily, but few frogs like them very much. Most frogs prefer flies of all sizes as their main food. Newly metamorphosed frogs eat fruit flies as well as aphids, small crickets, etc. The small to moderately sized frogs prefer

houseflies. Larger frogs prefer bluebottle flies. You can and should breed all of these flies during the winter, if you can't buy the maggots from a sport fishing shop. Breeding them, however, is usually associated with pungent, penetrating odors which are hardly tolerable in a home. In the summer it's easier: obtain a fly trap. (Do-it-yourself models are usually unsatisfactory.) Bait it with raw meat remnants or an old fish head and catch up to 200 flies a day.

Frogs won't disdain eating grasshoppers and crickets, as well as their larvae in all stages of development. In this case, home-breeding of these insects is not so smelly. The larger frogs such as *Litoria caerulea* and *Bufo marinus*, to name only a few, eat small chunks of meat (handed to them on long straws) as well as small mice, which you can easily breed yourself down in the cellar. Breeding of these "food animals" or "livestock" is not so difficult at all. Because a varied diet is a prime requirement for the well-being and reproductive capacities of our frogs, here are some details about the breeding of living foods.

The tiny fruitfly, *Drosophila melanogaster*, is the most important food insect for the smallest and youngest frogs. During the warm season they'll fly by themselves into a glass that contains pieces of fruit, and there you have your first breeding population! The maggots crawl out of the eggs (which have been laid in the glass) and later change into pupae, so cover the glass with gauze or a piece of nylon hosiery (stocking or pantyhose). At 77° F. room temperature the first fruit flies emerge. Now cool the whole glass and feed the flies to the frogs in the terrarium. Or put the benumbed flies, or perhaps only some of them, in another glass along with some fruit for food and breed more flies. There are many recipes for food for flies: brown bread and dates, sugar and yeast, banana mash, baby food, or many other sweet and nourishing food remnants. A pinch of an anti-mold product (your pet shop probably has it) keeps mold from growing on the fly food for the second usage, but after that make up a new one because by then mites and other tiny creatures start to appear. With the above methods, you can also breed the vestigial-winged mutant of the fruit fly.

The house fly (*Musca domestica*) takes three to four weeks to develop from egg to the imago (that is, the actual fly). Small and large frogs alike enjoy them. They can be bred at normal or slightly warmer-than-normal room temperature, although a larger glass or bottle (1 to 3 quarts) is needed. Cover it with wire mesh or gauze and close the access doorway with a wooden or metal slide. Catch your first breeders inside the house, not outside, otherwise you'll get big bluebottle flies, too. There are many recipes for the food: (1) rye bran with yeast and milk, (2) cow manure with sawdust, (3) rye bran with curds, and, later, as a supplement for the maggots, chopped meat or meat tidbits. Sawdust, straw and paper help the hatching flies to crawl out, but before using them as food for the frogs, build up their strength for several days by feeding them banana mash, milk, sugar, and a few drops of liquid vitamins, so that they make a nourishing meal for the frogs. If too many flies hatch at once, then keep some in the refrigerator for several days until you need them.

The larger bluebottle fly for feeding larger frogs is bred in a similar way, but with the difference that both the maggots and the flies are fed on meat. There is one significant disadvantage of fly-breeding that must be mentioned: the fermentation and ammoniacal odors associated with breeding small flies, plus the odor of rotting meat when breeding bluebottle flies, is devastating. Breeding of flies is recommended only away from areas in which you live. The somewhat more expensive method of buying fly maggots in a sport fishing shop is almost odorless; you keep them at 77^0 to about 80^0 F., then feed the hatchlings well with banana mash and vitamins several days before giving them to your frogs.

Other possibly suitable insects for frog food are the brownish-black Mediterranean cricket (*Gryllus bimaculatus*) and a light brown domestic one (*Gryllus domesticus*), which, unlike field crickets and grasshoppers in the temperate zone, can be bred all year. When newly hatched, these insects can be fed to the small frogs such as the Dendrobatids, the smaller marsh frogs and young frogs; when these newly hatched insects grow somewhat larger, they'll make a better meal for the larger frogs. These insects, along with flies, are the most important source of food, especially during the colder time of the year. The breeding bins have to be dry and well ventilated, easily cleaned, and completely closeable; otherwise you could be greeted one day by a din of chirping music all over the place and think you were not in a living room in the temperate zone, but out in the living jungle very much more to the sunny south. In my breeding set-up, there's an average room temperature of 86° F., and the temperature inside the breeding bins goes over 104° F. because of the light bulb I have burning there day and night (but just during breeding). These breeding bins have proved themselves successful over many years for breeding crickets and even grasshoppers, so I'd like to describe them here in more detail.

The framework (60 x 40 x 45 cm) is braced by gluing several slats underneath and on the back. Both sides and the top are covered with fine-mesh wire screening or coarse gauze that even the newly hatched crickets can't get through. The front side, which looks somewhat more complicated, has various functions. The largest portion is covered with the same wire screening, except for the opening for the Plexiglas or glass slide. This opening lets you reach in to pick out insects, clean up, and change the food bins.

The slide must, of course, work well enough to keep the cage closed and not let any insects escape. You could build a small hinged door instead of a slide, if more convenient.

The screening over the bottom should be of large enough mesh to let the wastes drop through, but small enough to keep the immature insects from falling or climbing through. All the wastes that fall through onto the metal tray underneath are easily disposed of. Newly hatched insects, however, tend to crawl through the screening. At this time, then, you could cover the screening with a board or a plastic tray filled with a layer of peat or sand. The newly hatched insects can't climb glass or smooth plastic walls. If you don't feed them right away to your frogs, then transfer them (along with their little paper shelters) soon to the rearing containers.

The cycle of development of these insects lasts from two to two and a half months. If you can keep two or three of these breeding cages in a dry, warm room, then you can breed all the desired sizes continuously. Crickets can be kept together if the cage is not too crowded, but the more agile species (the domestic, not the Mediterranean) eventually takes over.

The menu for crickets and grasshoppers is about the same: carrots, lettuce, and grass in summer, wheat germ in winter, plus fruit, clover, bread and mouse feed (pellets). Be careful with lettuce that's been sprayed with insecticide . . . it poisons your insects!

Continuous breeding requires uniform heat; breeding can come to a halt even 9° F. below the average temperature of 86° F. (95° F. for grasshoppers); 18° F. above the average (such as on a hot summer day in a greenhouse) is certain death. So a thermostat is desired for regulating heat and ventilation. You can transfer the bins to a very warm area, say a cellar with a furnace, a greenhouse, or near (or even on) a radiator (but verify its temperature first!). Or you can install an adjustable electric hot plate, preferably under the metal waste tray. Additionally, a continuous burning bulb in the cage overcomes the temperature highs and lows within the cage and provides a margin of safety in the event that the other heat sources fail.

The adult Mediterranean female cricket grows to about 3.3 cm, that of the domestic cricket to 2.3 cm. Females of the North American migratory grasshoppers are twice as large, that is, up to 5.3 cm (*Schistocerca peregrina*) and even up to 6 cm (*Locusta nigraforia*). These, too, do well in the breeding cage, although they prefer somewhat more green (and less dry) feed—more fresh grass and dandelion in summer, more wheat germ in winter. You can prepare wheat germ by spreading out wheat grains on moist newspaper. In a warm, moist and bright spot they'll germinate up to 10 cm. Small and moderately sized grasshoppers fed on these germinated wheat grains are relished by almost all frogs. Large adult grasshoppers are, of course, fare only for the large frogs such as *Litoria caerulea*. After a few years, egg-laying dwindles because of the constant inbreeding, then you've got the same problem you had in the beginning: how to build up a breeding population. The best solution is to trade breeders with other terrarium hobbyists. Hobbyist magazines and newsletters, too, often print traders' requests and offers as a service to promote the hobby. Or, you can simply collect your breeders whenever you are afield or on vacation.

The breeding of wax moths (such as *Achroea grisella* or *Galleria melonella*) is even simpler than for the insects described above. Just take a square plastic box with a tight lid (refrigerator containers about 20 x 20 x 10 cm), cut a vent (10 x 10 cm) into the lid and seal it with a square of fine screen (melted wax over rubberized or adhesive tape makes a good solder). Then you only need a breeding group of moths, half an old, empty honeycomb, and a slightly higher-than-normal room temperature. Breeding will go on automatically. If that's too slow for you, then place the breeding box in a warmer spot. You'll soon be overrun with moths! When the maggots have almost eaten through the wax of the honeycomb, place a fresh piece of honeycomb, wrapped in paper, inside. When the crumbly layer of maggot droppings gets too thick, clean out the whole cage, and use the maggots that are left as a new breeding group with another honeycomb.

To feed your frogs, place the breeding bins in the terrarium and then open the bins to let the moths fly out into the frog's world. Or you can put corrugated cardboard or little paper rolls in the bins so that the maggots can crawl in, and from which you can pick them out easier than you can from the wax in the honeycomb. Maggots are good for various other amphibians, monkeys and birds, too, as well as for the forced feeding of sick frogs or for the diet of convalescing frogs. Don't forget to add vitamins to your home-bred insects' food, or at least give it to the frogs along with the insects. Various liquid and powdered vitamin preparations are available at pet shops. Insects caught out in nature are usually more nutritious, whether flies, the "plankton" you can catch up in an insect net out in the fields, earthworms, snails, butterflies, or wood lice, which many frogs like. But the aquatic frogs, certain *Pipa* species and clawed frogs have other tastes, such as for tubifex worms, guppies and bits of beef heart. Be sure to remove everything that's not eaten up, for it starts to smell quite bad after awhile. Take care not to let your insects or frogs escape . . . neighbors may object and even sue you, especially if your moths get into their woolens!

This section, of course, can't cover the great variety of live foods and their propagation in great detail as comprehensively and minutely as a larger work devoted specifically to that topic. For thoroughness of treatment, perhaps you can obtain a copy of *The Encyclopedia of Live Foods*, published by T.F.H. Publications.

Xenopus laevis, the African clawed frog, is used as a laboratory animal for pregnancy tests and dissection in the U. S. because the local *Rana pipiens* is getting scarce. The pustules on the legs and flanks of this hylid frog (below) from Mexico, *Pachymedusa dacnicolor,* are not indications of a parasitic condition but are normal growths characteristic of the species.

Ailments

"An ounce of prevention is worth a pound of cure." This is as true for frogs as for people. But how does one *prevent?*

1. Wash your hands after each time you handle a frog. This protects both you and the other frogs in case the frog you handle has a communicable disease.
2. Try to quarantine new frogs longer than the eight to twelve weeks suggested later. Perhaps two to three months is ideal for stopping transmission of disease.
3. Don't give insects or other food refused by one group of frogs to another group.

4. Wash out utensils before transferring them from one terrarium to another. If you disinfect them, be sure to wash all the disinfectant off before filling with food.
5. Once or twice weekly is not too often to clean out a terrarium. Remove droppings from walls and glass panes, plants and the ground; take out any old skins shed by the frogs.
6. Change bath water daily if possible.

Cleanliness helps reduce bacterial and parasitic diseases. Heavy worm infestation can cause intestinal prolapse, a condition frequently seen in tree frogs. Too cramped a terrarium and lack of ample space for movement can also lead to health problems. Veterinary help is expensive, and not all vets know about frogs; in fact, very few vets would probably know more than you after you studied up on your particular frog species. The veterinarian, however, might help you with parasitological examination of your frog's droppings.

Since I'm neither a veterinarian nor a parasitologist, I can only pass on to you what I've learned from discussions, autopsies, and examinations made by a specialist (the director of the parasitology department of an important university) over many years. The following are the most important diseases, how to recognize them, and, if possible, how to treat the frogs for them.

Mechanical injuries: Skin damage, bite wounds, etc., can fester, which is serious for frogs. Sulfonamide ointment or powder, especially the newer preparations that are effective against many different microbes, are available at pet shops.

Skin changes are easily recognizable because they may be caused by parasites such as certain mites. Better let the specialist try to remove them, although a specialist may be quite hard to find. Products are available for topical application (powder ointment, liquids).

"Tumors" of various kinds grow on amphibians, too, although mostly in the inner organs, so these are hard to spot and treat.

Crooked limbs and rickets are usually due to poor maintenance. Calcium and vitamin D, along with ultraviolet light, may help if the condition is not too advanced.

Poor appetite and weakness can have many causes (internal fungal disease, amphibian tuberculosis, etc.) which are hardly curable. Amebiasis, a parasitic infection of the internal organs, may be cleared up with various products, such as a terramycin solution.

Intestinal prolapse may be cured in its initial stages with a product that rids the frog of its nematodes (parasitic worms).

Bloody enteritis or colitis, a bacterial disease, is recognizable from traces of blood in the droppings. Small doses of sulfanilamide (0.5 gram/liter of water) may help, at least during the early stages.

Ascites or swelling up of the body (dropsy), probably caused by certain bacteria, doesn't have any cure as far as I know. The same is true for blindness.

Paralysis, too, is hardly curable, except perhaps in the initial stages of mild cases. Paralysis caused by poisoning, however, may be helped by repeated bathing of the victim in clean water. Because all amphibians have a more or less powerful venom in their skin, mass shipment of these creatures often leads to such paralysis. Ideally, each animal should be shipped separately.

An unidentified *Atelopus* sp. with very beautiful and intricate markings.

The Australian tree frog *Litoria caerulea* resembles externally the Mexican tree frog *Pachymedusa dacnicolor* illustrated earlier.

Edema or swollen parts of the body can be treated in the early stages of the disease by a varied diet that includes a multivitamin preparation, usually available at pet shops.

External fungal infections should be seen by a specialist because some of these fungi can cause infections in human beings, too.

Fatty liver is a frequent metabolic disease, the causes of which are still uncertain. Fat deposition in the liver can so burden that organ that the frog's death is unavoidable. This disease is best recognized, unfortunately, upon autopsy.

Salmonellosis, caused by bacteria, is easily transmitted from animal to animal. . .or to human beings when hygienic measures do not govern your handling of sick frogs. If a specialist diagnoses this disease for you, you can try to cure the frog with a broad-spectrum antibiotic like chloromycetin (= chloramphenicol).

The causes of many parasitic infections include one-celled animals (protozoans, such as the ameba, which cause amebic dysentery and amebiasis), nematodes (roundworms), mites, and perhaps even a mixture of several of these organisms. So rational treatment often requires an exact diagnosis of just what organisms must be eliminated; certain drugs may kill only certain parasites but not the others. You'll need the help of a friend with a microscope (in the worst case), or a veterinarian, parasitologist, microbiologist, or even your family physician if he or she cares to take the time and effort to name the parasites for you, then tell you what drugs, if any, might eliminate them.

After every death of a frog, thoroughly clean out the container with a disinfectant. Watch closely for the slightest signs of disease in the survivors.

An albino *Rana catesbeiana*. In nature albinism can be considered an abnormality because albinos are easy prey for other animals.

Phrynohyas venulosa (upper photo) is a large tree frog from Central America. It has a very thick glandular skin on the back which secretes mucus copiously to help prevent desiccation. Madagascar has some very rare frogs that are seldom seen in captivity. The tomato frog, *Dyscophus antongilli (lower photo), is one of them.*

49

Dendrobates histrionicus is so variable that finding two individuals which are exactly alike in color and markings is not easy. *Bufo melanostictus* (below) originates from Southeast Asia. These toads have countless warts which are pointed or spiny. Note the parotoid gland behind the eye.

Obtaining Frogs

Before you bring your frogs home, you (theoretically at least) should have a balanced terrarium and an ongoing breeding of insects ready and waiting. Unfortunately, such preparations are rarely so complete. You might suddenly decide upon a "once-in-a-lifetime" buy at the pet shop . . . where the salespeople may not even know the name of the rare animal they're selling to you. So only after you buy do you really learn anything about the creature and just how you have to feed it. This usually takes some library research. While you run around looking for the proper food

(perhaps from another hobbyist), give your frog at least both bath water and a comfortable warmth, both of which should keep it (if it's healthy) a day or so until you discover what it eats and until you round up enough of it. Hopefully you did pick out a healthy frog at the pet shop.

Here are some rules of thumb for frog health when shopping:

1. Shiny, tightly fitting skin.
2. Rounded angles, no sunken areas (at least where there shouldn't be any) where the bones stick out.
3. Each limb flexible, well-formed and straight (at least where it's supposed to be); abnormally bent and lame limbs are evidence of rickets.
4. Unbroken skin all the way to the tip of the snout. (Broken skin may be the result of injuries caused by the frog's leaping against the cage walls . . . or caused by fungal disease.)
5. Good reflexes: when you touch the frog or push it somewhat from behind, it should do *something*, such as jump or otherwise show life . . . yet, it can also play dead, a typical fear reaction. By the way, never handle frogs when you have open wounds on your hands. Wash your hands immediately after you handle a frog, toad and the like. Some people may be allergic. And if the frog or toad happens to be one with venom in its skin, it could get into your bloodstream (if you have open wounds on your hands) and perhaps even cause some temporary paralysis.

Ideally, it's best to capture your own tropical frogs. Then you'd have to provide sufficient moisture, ventilation, tidbits of food and cleanliness en route. Don't keep too many frogs or toads in one container; frogs and toads may be poisoned, either by body contact with other frogs and toads or by eating them.

If you ever do bring home tropical frogs which you caught in the wild, or even when you buy new ones at the pet shop, keep the new arrivals in quarantine for about eight to twelve weeks. Then, if you don't see evidence of any disease (you could have the droppings analyzed by a parasitologist or microbiologist), put them with your other frogs. This is no absolute guarantee of the health of later generations from these specimens, but is a great guarantee for the immediate well-being of your terrarium or aquarium. I once shortened the quarantine time because of my impatience and suffered the consequences. The new arrival infected all of my other frogs with a fungal disease and wiped out my whole terrarium. Remember that home-bred frogs may be weaker or less survival-oriented than wild ones and are certainly not immune to many of the diseases of wild frogs, who may tolerate and live quite passably with some disease which would kill the more delicate home-bred ones.

An aquarium for fully aquatic frogs.

A terrarium for savanna-dwelling frogs.

A female *Pedostibes hosii*, a divergent type of toad from Malaysia. Males differ in appearance from the females in this species. A male and female *Rhacophorus leucomystax* (below) in breeding position or amplexus.

Breeding

Can tropical frogs be bred at all in a terrarium, or are there insurmountable obstacles? Well, if you've gotten your frogs through everything we've covered up to now, then you certainly should give breeding a try. It's somewhat tricky perhaps to inspire a frog—one you know quite well—to reproduce, but here is where the terrarium keeper is forced into research . . . which often takes the sensitivity of an artist. That's why zoos usually let you know right away when they've succeeded in breeding; wild animals do not always breed so easily in captivity. Your time, expenses and efforts are soon forgotten when you succeed in

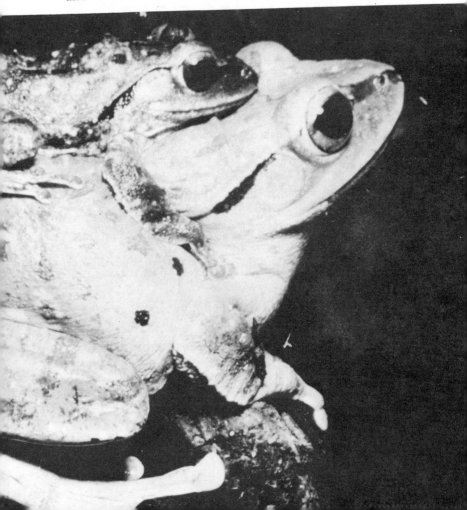

breeding your frogs . . . perhaps even on into the third or fourth generation. Patience is the prime virtue for this kind of work. Whoever thinks a technically sophisticated and perfected terrarium permits you to breed many frogs in little time (or even to turn a neat profit by sales!), will surely be disappointed. Home-breeding, however, is often necessitated because of the restrictions on the importation and exportation of exotic species (which tropical frogs are indeed) in some places where nature conservation is practiced.

Frog-breeding requires males *and* females, for asexual reproduction does not normally occur, as far as we know, in the frog world. The sexes are not always easy to differentiate. Usually, but not always, males have one or two vocal sacs and croak sort of sullenly when held leaning backwards against the heel of your hand. The adult females are almost always larger than the males. Often, such as in the group of dendrobatids, the males have thicker fingertips. Otherwise the external sexual characteristics are not as easily recognized as they are in mammals. A male-female pair is often not recognized until the two frogs engage in mating behavior. Whoever wishes to breed frogs based upon these vague guidelines has to start with several animals to allow for acquisition of experience and to allow a certain probability to develop—the more frogs, the more chance of reproduction. Various successful breeding results are described below as a sort of inspiration to personally witness the big moment in any terrarium keeper's life.

The small aquatic web-footed *Hemipipa carvalhoi* of the family of tongueless frogs, the Pipidae, is easily kept in an aquarium (50 x 30 x 25 cm). The water temperature should be between 68° and about 77° F. I was successful with tap water (from Lake Constance, in Europe) of 9° to 14° DH hardness and pH 7 to 8. A set-up should include a niche for shelter.

Breeding of these frogs runs smoothly and is such an interesting avocation that it should be tried often. The frogs usually stay on the bottom of the aquarium, moving about with short backward swimming movements and coming up to the surface only for air. They try to shovel in with their stiffly held arms and outstretched fingers everything that's not securely anchored. They spit out any little stones that happen to get raked in by accident, but quickly swallow tubifex, insects, tiny fish or little pieces of beef heart. Within a day from when the male begins his slowly rising trill to audibly announce his readiness to mate, the mature female everts her cloaca like a small tube, then the real nuptial dance starts. The male first embraces his partner around the hips, whereby the female's back feet tremble. Then they both slowly somersault through the whole aquarium. Only when this circular performance is achieved does the male raise himself somewhat from his mate as she releases the first eggs from her cloaca. These eggs don't drop down through the water but land on the edge of her back, just over the cloaca. The male now presses himself up flat against the back of the female and pushes the eggs, with alternating movements of each of his back legs, all the way forward on the female's back, probably fertilizing them at the same time. They repeat this ritual several times. The black female looks as if she were covered with hailstones, which are, of course, 60 to 125 white eggs (each about 2mm), all nearly lined up in ranks and glued to her back. In two days' time most of the eggs have sunken into her skin, and only a few spots remain to remind us of the nuptial whiteness.

Three weeks later, little bumps swell up on her back, and the tadpoles break out of these sacs. They wiggle loose of the craters, make it up to the surface for a moment, then sink down to the bottom. And that's the most dangerous time during their short larval life. If you don't get them out of the aquarium immediately, they'll be gobbled up by their parents, to whom the tadpoles taste just as good as guppies. Not many of the tadpoles hatch from the eggs and crawl out of their mother's back. Of 110 eggs on the female's back, only about 25 reach tadpole-hood. Were the other eggs absorbed into the skin or were they part of the food used by the surviving larvae during their embryonic development? There are still many such questions waiting to be answered. The transparent larvae grow fast in water which is not too cool (about 75° to 79° F.) and into which you sprinkle powdered food, but they remain transparent for quite a while longer.

In about eight weeks the back legs appear, and in another two weeks the front legs. The body is then 1.5 cm long and the tail is its longest when it reaches about 3 cm, but begins to disappear during the ten days following that. The young frog is capable of reproduction in eight months. The female is ready to lay eggs again about a week or two after the tadpoles are "born," and it seems that the male—with his trilling announcement that he's ready to mate—is waiting for her. Because too many females may interfere with one another during mating, a good breeding group for the small aquarium mentioned above consists of one male and two females. With less sexually mature frogs you can observe the mating procedure better and, above all, save the tadpoles by fishing them out before they're eaten. This mating behavior of the dwarf web-footed toad (which grows to about 5.5 cm) is similar to that of the other pipids and clawed frogs (xenopids), and the development of the tadpoles is similar. The young frogs, like their parents, eat tubifex, fly larvae, and even guppy fry.

The brightly colored dendrobatids make up quite an interesting family. The Indians poison their hunting arrows and darts with the venom in the skin of these tiny (2.4 cm) frog midgets—all fascinating creatures with their bright reds, greens, blacks, yellows, and blues, and also because of their breeding habits. These splotches of color can really be called the diamonds among the frogs, especially when you see them sitting around on the dark green foliage all day long. But these real inhabitants of the tropical rainforest need a relative humidity of 80 to 100% and a temperature of 68° to about 82° F. Only then do they feel comfortable enough to annihilate unexpectedly huge quantities of freshly hatched crickets, fruit flies and the tiny "plankton" that abounds in the vegetation around them . . . and only then can you count on their reproducing.

Mating behavior is about the same for all of them, so I'll give only one example here, the golden tree frog, *Dendrobates auratus*. I obtained 300 offspring from a breeding group of one male and two females over a period of 31 months. Finally, after five years in my terrarium, the male (you can recognize the male by his thicker fingertips) came to the end of his quite successful frog's existence. He was successful because the results of his "activities" went on for two- and one-half years: 75 batches of three to nine eggs had to be fertilized during this time. The male watched over the eggs, at least at first, because the female didn't leave her eggs in the water, but put them on a bromeliad leaf which both the male and female had picked out beforehand. With her laying of the eggs, the female does her part for posterity, leaving it to the male to sit on the eggs during the next half an hour so he can fertilize them. As many as four times a day during the following days he climbs up alone on the bromeliad leaf and moistens the eggs.

In about fourteen days he's supposed to take the wriggling embryos on his back and into the water. . .but my male never did that. The embryos either slid back into the leaf concavity or else wriggled over the leaftip and into the water container underneath. The parents or other frogs would have soon eaten them up if I had not carefully pushed them with my finger into a small plastic bowl, filled it with water so the tiny creatures could swim, and covered it with a plastic lid to reduce evaporation. The embryonic development of all dentrobatids probably proceeds similarly, as described below.

First, the so-called primitive streak or neural groove, which later becomes the spinal cord, forms on the fertilized eggs. Then this groove develops further into an embryo, which shows up visibly as a tiny bump on the fourth day. Two days later you can see the external gill branches degenerate or atrophy, first on the right then on the left side. You can see the embryo moving by the sixth day, and from then on the movements become stronger and more frequent. The embryo's membranous sac keeps on growing, too, until it thins out and bursts about the fifteenth day, liberating a brand new tadpole who can now seek out its own food.

The tadpoles are transferred to another tank with a water level of 1 to 2 cm, which is later increased to 5 to 8 cm when the tadpoles are somewhat larger. Finely flaked food is sprinkled over the surface of the water. The tadpoles manage quite well to gobble up the food particles. The hindlegs take about seven to twelve weeks to grow, and the front legs take another two to three weeks to appear. During the following weeks these "larvae" undergo a miraculous transformation or metamorphosis whereby their aquatic nature changes to that of a land animal which now breathes oxygen from the air instead of absorbing it from the water. During this metamorphosis, the tadpole's mouth changes into a frog's mouth, so these in-between tadpole-frog creatures cannot eat.

The young frog's tail is absorbed over the next six days until it disappears, and you've got a brand new little frog at the water's edge in your aquarium, waiting for a chance to climb up on dry land. If, however, this tiny 1-cm long, green-black speckled frog got out into the dry world around his aquarium, it would mean certain death for him. So it's advisable to take him out several days *before* he reaches this stage (that is, while he still has a remnant of his tail) and transfer him to a moss-padded terrarium. Don't forget to put a flat water pan or jar lid in, too, so he can satisfy his moisture needs by bathing whenever he wants to. You can also sink a pan of freshly hatched crickets down in the moss layer, and perhaps shake in some vestigial-winged fruit flies, too. Your frogs will immediately grasp the fact that this wriggling, fluttering mass means food. In a week I usually transfer the young frogs into the terrarium with the older frogs. At first the young ones hide in holes and corners, but they soon start hopping around with the others, taking maggots, small crickets, fruit flies, and other tiny insects from the feeding pan.

The dendrobatids include the genera *Colostethus* and *Phyllobates* (or leaf climber) as well as the *Dendrobates* genus. In the leaf climbers, too, the males initiate the mating process by repeatedly emitting minute-long trills at a somewhat higher pitch than those emitted by *Dendrobates auratus*, or something like the singing exercises of a young male canary. Then the males follow the females and try to stroke them with one hand or to jump up on them, hopping along together throughout the whole terrarium until they've selected a suitable breeding place on a bromeliad leaf. They may also be quite satisfied with the smooth surface of a petri dish (a round flat dish used to grow bacterial and fungal cultures in laboratories). The female lays three to ten eggs. Don't let their tiny size compared with that of the golden tree frog (*Dendrobates auratus*) frighten you.

Although the fully grown *Phyllobates lugubris* is just as big as *Dendrobates auratus*, the eggs are only half the diameter. The development of the embryos and tadpoles up to the frog stage is the same as for the *D. auratus*, except that the young frogs are half as large as those of *D. auratus*. As an experiment, I raised them together and learned that the young *Phyllobates lugubris* took a year to catch up in size to their cousins, who were of the same age. It's an exquisite experience to watch such a tiny minifrog—perhaps only 1 cm long and already sporting the same coloration as its elders—hopping around peacefully with the others in the terrarium.

Many hylids, such as, for example, the red-eyed frog, *Agalychnis callidryas,* are like dendrobatids in that the males are smaller than the females, which seldom reach 7.5 cm. These Central American rainforest frogs—with their brilliant red eyes, hands and feet, a usually bluish stripe on the sides, and a leafy green body color, are amont the most attractive species of the very large family of tree frogs. Breeding has often been successful with these frogs, too, so we'll mention it briefly.

Egg-laying is preceded by a week-long engagement, during which the male rides around uninterruptedly on his future mate's back. His diet during this time is somewhat restricted, as they both have to dine on what the female manages to catch of the various flies in the terrarium. . .and she has to catch them with the male riding around on her back. One fine evening the female picks out a large leaf hanging over the water and attaches her foamy cache of eggs to the underside of the leaf. In barely a week's time the gelatinous clump, along with its wriggling embryos, drops off and falls into the water container underneath. Because the embryos swim free in a few days, it's best to transfer them to an aquarium. Add an antifungal agent to the water because it's just at this time that fungal infection of these creatures is greatest. Feed them flaked food and lettuce on the surface of the water, from where they'll munch on it. These frog larvae don't swim around as wildly as other frog larvae, but hold themselves at about a 45° angle in the water. From their 1 cm length they grow to 5 cm during the next five to seven weeks, then, as young frogs, start at once to catch fruit flies and house flies. At first only the ruby eyes and intense body green reflect the beauty of their parents, but later their red hands and feet and the stripes along their sides show up.

The pouched frog, *Gastrotheca marsupiata*, has an interesting way of rearing its young. The word "pouch" could be somewhat misleading, for it's not like a kangaroo's belly pocket, but rather a knapsack on its back. The males of these tree frogs of the Central American rainforest, too, are smaller than the females, but make up for their small size by croaking all the louder! You may miss observing the process of fertilization because of the shorter duration of the night, compared with the duration of daylight, but you'll soon see, perhaps one fine morning, that a happy event has occurred during the night: the skin on the female's back stretches out over many boil-like bumps. Shortly after you see a lot of movement in these bumps, meaning the mother frog is just about finished with the care of the brood. She moves to the edge of the water basin in the terrarium and uses a toe of one of her hind feet to widen the small opening at the lower part of her back, letting one tadpole after another hatch out into the water. Of the 100 or so tadpoles who come into the world like this, that is, drop into the water, there are always a few casualties. The frog mother may even bring out a dead embryo or even yolk the following day when she scrapes around with the longest toe on her hindfoot in the opening of her knapsack-like pocket; she does this to clean it out in preparation for the next brood. Our real task begins now, because caring for 100 active and greedy tadpoles requires a bit of work—not so much work in feeding them as keeping their water clean, which rapidly gets dirty. There are certain limits in raising frogs, for although frog hobbyists may have a well-made terrarium for the little ones, they often lack all the aquaria and filters so necessary for the numerous offspring to reach the metamorphosis stage; the weaker ones succumb when too many are kept too closely together.

In captivity, under the same conditions, all tadpoles usually take seven weeks up to metamorphosis, but can take as long as five months. I found this out not only for the larvae of many other frogs, but also for my pouched frogs; this doesn't mean, however, that the latecomers are weaker or more susceptible than the "first born" frogs. The same thing is true for African marsh frogs of the genus *Hyperolius*. There are probably about 170 different species of these lively little fellows who live in the savannahs as well as near tranquil bodies of water. And the numerous members of all of these different species contribute to a rather heavy population of frogs. My own experience has shown me that there are no particular obstacles to keeping and breeding them, and, in captivity, a female can produce not only 100 but up to 800 tadpoles a year. The marbled marsh frog, *Hyperolius marmoratus*, along with the well known and likewise prolific *Rhacophorus leucomystax*, belong to the "rowing" or paddling family Rhacophoridae, the Old World tree frogs.

The black-white-yellow marbled pattern on the back contrasts richly with the red legs and foot soles, although color tones and patterns vary considerably. About Christmastime the male blows up his vocal sac quite formidably, almost as large as the 3 cm frog itself. His croaking call—a short hard *d-i-e-t d-i-e-t*—is loud and piercing . . . quite suitable for attracting the females as well as impressing other males in his vicinity. The males, inflating themselves and croaking threateningly, jump aggressively at each other much as the males of other animals often do. During their mating season these males pay scant attention to eating. One evening the frog couple sits down at the water's edge or on a floating water plant. . .and in the morning you can count over 400 tiny blue-green eggs, and often, a week later, another 300 from the same female. Almost all the eggs are fertilized and, if the water is clean, they won't be attacked by fungi, which all means that your biggest problem is to provide enough aquarium space to put up all of these hatching tadpoles so that they don't damage one another. Although I've never seen any active cannibalism, when the weaker tadpoles die and float around for a few days in the water, the others will nibble at them. You can feed these growing tadpoles (they grow from 7 to 51 mm) with flake food during their one and one-half to six-month development. Your froglets—feeding on fruit flies then on house flies—can reach froghood and sexual maturity in ten months' time. Then the cycle keeps on . . . my own frogs are now fourth generation ones which I raised in captivity.

The peaked or pointed frog, *Megophrys nasuta*, gets its name from its skin folds which project like horse blinders out over its eyes and nose. This relatively large ground frog (males grow to 9 cm and females to 16 cm) is best kept in a large, flat terrarium. These moisture-loving frogs prefer about 8 cm of water (at about 72° F.) in their terrarium. Their Spartan but sanitary household consists of a synthetic foam platform and a piece of cork float, plus some *Scindapsus* and *Philodendron* plants. *Megophrys* likes a general temperature of about 72° F. and a diet of crickets, earthworms and newly born mice. Mating, when it comes, usually occurs after you've changed the water. The embracing part is followed by the deposition of eggs, partially in the water and partially at the edge of the cork float near the water. From these 2 mm eggs hatch about 6 mm wriggling larvae, which have to be transferred to an aquarium. They hang down at first in long strings from the surface of the water or from the piece of cork, then swim free a day later. When you sprinkle finely ground dry food on the surface of the water, the tadpoles come along and scoop it up in their funnel-like mouths. You can see the hind feet starting to bud from the 17th day on; then in another nine days the forelimbs start to bud. Lower your water level now down to 3 cm so your froglets don't drown. In another week the tail stump is almost gone, and the 1 cm young frogs can be

Dendrobates auratus (with green and black pattern) and *Phyllobates lugubris* (black and gold), two poison-arrow frogs.

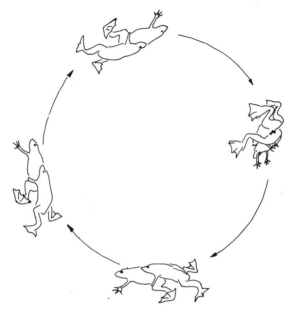

Nuptial dance of the dwarf pipid *Hemipipa carvalhoi*.

Development of the tadpole and the changing of the mouth during metamorphosis of *Dendrobates auratus*.

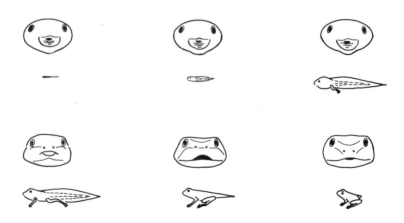

transferred to the rearing terrarium. The foam layer, which you keep constantly moist, guarantees a high air humidity as well as helps your frogs to catch all the little insects you put into the terrarium as frog food. Fed in this way, plus a twice-weekly supplement of a calcium-vitamin preparation, the little frogs quickly grow to double their size in one and one-half months.

Development of the embryo of *Dendrobatus auratus*.

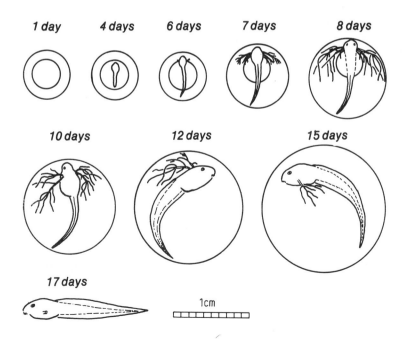

Dendrobates leucomelas, a brightly colored dendrobatid with iridescent skin.

Bufo blombergi is a large toad eight to ten inches long. This Colombian toad was only described as recently as 1951. The red toad, *Bufo carens* (below),from Kenya, Zaire and southern Africa, distinguishes itself from other African *Bufo* by lacking external parotoid glands, having a typanum as large as the eye and by a black dorsolateral ridge.

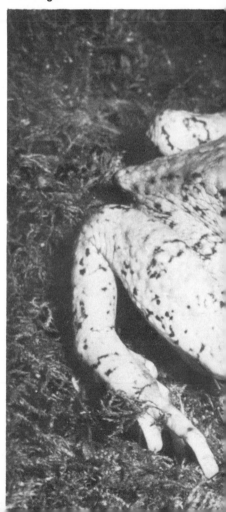

Toads

Many terrarium hobbyists prefer toads. These tranquil, prudent animals, with their large, attentive, almost sad eyes, come out of hiding in the evening. They soon become tame and eat out of your hand.

The Colombian giant toad, *Bufo blombergi*, discovered in 1950, quickly awakened the interest of the pet industry, zoos and animal lovers. These toads don't have the usual warty skin of other toads, but rather a smooth, rusty reddish brown skin. Their food is the same as for *Megophrys nasuta*, but, because of their enormous size (females can at-

Dendrobates histrionicus appears in many varieties. The markings may be spots or bands in blue, yellow or red on a brown to black background.

Reed frogs (upper photo) come in innumerable colors and markings. *Hyperolius marmoratus taeniatus* (lower photo), the black-and-white striped reed frog from southeastern Africa.

tain 27 cm), they can also make a meal of fully grown mice. These toads like a high humidity and should have a large water pan (with water at a temperature of about 77° F.) or else have half of their terrarium built as a water basin. The male's croaking call announces open mating season, and soon strings of eggs—from one to six rows—appear in the water. We can only estimate the number of eggs (unless you want to count them all!) at up to 15,000 from each female. When these are all fertilized, your problem will be to provide adequate aquaria or other containers. But Mother Nature intervenes: many eggs succumb to fungal infection, so that some of the mother toads have "only" about 2,000 tadpoles left, which grow from the 2 mm eggs over the course of the next eight days. After you've changed the water (which you should do) they wriggle around on the bottom awhile but soon recover and swim to the sides of the aquarium and carry on nicely, slurping in their dry feed. Their metabolism is quite high, so nitrites accumulate in the water so fast that you really need frequent water changes despite filter and intense aeration. In about two weeks the hind legs bud and in another twenty days the forelegs, too. A week later the 1 cm, darkly speckled toads leave their moist native element. The young giant toads are a credit to their name of "giant toad," for a few of these toads, bred in captivity by a certain A.A. Schmidt and also cared for by me, kept on growing at a monthly rate of 1 cm in length and width! But it certainly won't go on like that indefinitely; these animals are now seven months old and they'll soon reach their maximum size.

Two toads from the dry, southwesten United States and adjacent Mexico: *Bufo punctatus* (upper photo) and *Bufo debilis* (lower photo). These toads are small in size, have a very short larval development after strong rains and lead a burrowing life at other times.

Rhacophorus leucomystax,
a common South Asian tree frog.

A hylid frog photographed on the surface of a sheet of glass. Note the suction-like area created between the ventral surface of the frog and the glass enabling it to cling on very smooth surfaces. The claws of the hind limb of the African clawed frog, *Xenopus laevis* (below), are visible in this photo. These frogs, although imported in numbers in many states, are banned in California; they are carnivorous, very prolific and can destroy the native frog fauna.

Identification

While certain species are protected by law, these efforts at natural conservation and ecological protection can only succeed if people are able to clearly identify the species of their pets! This thought, once formally expressed by perhaps one of the greatest herpetologists, Professor Robert Mertens, leads us to talk a bit (but not too much) about the scientific classification of frogs based upon the *International Rules of Zoological Nomenclature*, which also apply to all other animals as well. Each animal is assigned a genus name and a species name, such as *Dyscophus antongilli*, the tomato frog. Sometimes a third name is added for a subspecies or race, such as *Hyperolius marmoratus taeniatus*. Unfortunately, common English names do not always exist for some of the rarer tropical frogs.

Dyscophus antongilli is bright orange red, leading to its common name of tomato frog.

An immature *Bufo blombergi* (2 centimeters in length) showing the juvenile pattern.

Identification of frogs is really not too difficult . . . you think at first. Usually (but not always) toads are warty, plump, rather large and prefer running on all fours or hopping prudently instead of leaping. But there are giant toads 24 cm long with smooth skin on their back, and there are mini-editions 2 cm long with warts. Tree frogs (Hylidae) generally have smooth skin with broadened fingertips and toes which reinforce the ability of the bottom side of the body to stick to things. But these characteristics also show up in another quite different family, the Rhacophoridae. Although tree frogs and the Rhacophoridae climb and leap about on grass and bushes, a large majority of frogs stay mainly on the ground, covering great distances if necessary by leaping. Some frogs have specialized digging tubercles on their strong feet, and so can dig into the more or less hard soil during dry periods. Others are web-footed, and can live in water or right on the edge of bodies of water. Despite similar external appearances and living habits, frogs can belong to quite different families. These unarmored creatures have a variable temperature (unlike, for example, a human being who must keep his body temperature within a few degrees of 98.6° F. or perish). They inhabit all parts of the world except the polar regions, so this adaptability stands them in good stead. Because the evolutionary development of various kinds of frogs led to similar body forms, behavior, pupil shape, finger and toe forms, and skin peculiarities, they cannot always be clearly differentiated by these external characteristics alone. Science, however, has provided other indications for differentiating and thus classifying them, but these indicators are not all recognizable externally. The internal structure of the chest and pelvis and the number and shape of the vertebrae are examples of these indicators.

The order Anura, to which the frogs belong, is divided into six suborders. The first four suborders include the more primitive frogs (those lower on the evolutionary scale). The last two suborders include the more advanced frogs (those higher on the evolutionary scale), their chief characteristic being that they no longer have ribs. Here is how the six orders are categorized:

Order: **ANURA** or **SALIENTIA** (classification according to Grzimek)
    Suborder 1: AMPHICOELA (Primitive frogs)
      Family: **Leiopelmatidae** (New Zealand primitive frogs)
      Family: **Ascaphidae** (Tailed frogs)
    Suborder 2: AGLOSSA (Tongueless frogs)
      Family: **Pipidae**
    Suborder 3: OPISTHOCOELA
      Family: **Discoglossidae** (Disc-tongued frogs)
      Family: **Rhinophrynidae** (Proboscis frogs)
    Suborder 4: ANOMOCOELA
      Family: **Pelobatidae** (Spadefoot Toads)
      Family: **Pelodytidae** (Mud divers)
    Suborder 5: DISPLASIOCOELA (True frogs and relatives)
      Family: **Ranidae** (True frogs)
        Subfamily: Arthroleptinae
        Subfamily: Sooglossinae
        Subfamily: Dendrobatinae
        Subfamily: Astylosterninae
        Subfamily: Phrynopsinae
        Subfamily: Raninae
        Subfamily: Petropedetinae
        Subfamily: Platymantinae
        Subfamily: Hemisinae
        Subfamily: Mantellinae

The tree frog *Agalychnis moreletii,* from northern Central America, has a brownish skin color at night and a green color during the daytime.

Leptodactylus fallax, a giant South American bullfrog, is called mountain hen by the natives.

Family: **Rhacophoridae** (Old World tree frogs)
Family: **Microhylidae** (Narrow-mouthed frogs)
    Subfamily: Dyscophinae
    Subfamily: Cophylinae
    Subfamily: Asterophryninae
    Subfamily: Sphenophryninae
    Subfamily: Microhylinae
    Subfamily: Brevicipinae
    Subfamily: Melanobatrachinae
Family: **Phrynomeridae**
Suborder 6: PROCOELA (Toads, tree frogs and their relatives)
    Family: **Pseudidae** (Harlequin frogs)
    Family: **Bufonidae** (True toads)
    Family: **Atelopodidae** (Atelopodid toads)
    Family: **Hylidae** (Tree frogs)
    Family: **Leptodactylidae** (Southern frogs)
        Subfamily: Liptodactylinae
        Subfamily: Rhinodermatinae
        Subfamily: Elosiinae
        Subfamily: Heleophryninae
        Subfamily: Cycloraninae
        Subfamily: Myobatrachinae
    Family: **Centrolenidae** (Glass frogs)

The chiromantid tree frogs are unusual because they have opposable fingers and thus grasp branches and twigs. This *Chiromatis petersii* (upper photo) was collected in Somalia, Africa. *Rana erythraea* (lower photo), from Southeast Asia has red colored tympanum.

Rana erythraea, the red-eared frog of Southeast Asia.

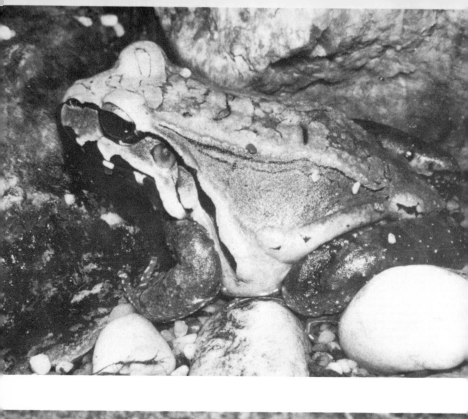

Conservation

In some countries, certain frogs and frog-like creatures are protected by law. If it were only a case of capturing frogs from a *naturally* kept habitat, there would be no problem, for frogs reproduce admirably well and prolifically. But man's encroachment (with deadly poisons and water-depleting construction) makes some effort desirable to promote the continuation of certain endangered species in the face of increasing pressure from man's transformation of the face of the earth. By our concern as frog hobbyists in keeping and breeding these wonderful creatures, we certainly contribute to the fight to preserve our animal life. Most people who might be overcritical at first of our making "pets" of these frogs often realize, when shown the great efforts we take for the wellbeing and breeding of our little friends, that we are indeed acting in a responsible manner and certainly do not belong in the same category as "nature destroyers and polluters." We are, as hobbyists, doing our part in conserving wildlife.

Overexploitation of a species commercially can easily endanger a species. *Leptodactylus pentadactylus* from South America is very much in demand for its legs as food and may disappear unless protected (upper photo). A species that is found in a very limited habitat can also disappear when its habitat is destroyed by housing developments. Such is the case with the black toad, *Bufo exsul,* found in a single valley in California (lower photo).